To the two most important women in my life:

Mom, thank you for teaching me to never give up on my dreams.
And, Jenny, my wife, thank you for allowing me to pursue those dreams.

Acknowledgements

I would like to thank all the young people of the quilting industry for their friendship and willingness to help, but more importantly for their passion for the new, the different, and the less than traditional. Just to name a few:

Valori Wells
For your trust and encouragement to slow down and perfect my art.

Amy Butler
For the encouraging words, kind personality and for reminding me to stop thinking so much and just ride.

Nicole deLeon & Phillip deLeon, Alexander Henry Fabrics
For an amazing eye for design, and a great sense of humor.

Shannon Mullen
For your countless hours of research and dedication to getting in touch with the next generation of sewers.

Scott Fox, Kim Novak, Sara Boughner and Team Pfaff
For your belief in me and for allowing me to sell the best machines on the planet!

Michael Miller Fabrics
Thanks for the picture perfect prints for my quilts of paradise.

Amber Howe
For being there every step of the way.

Kristen,
Make Some Waves
Rob Appell 2011

Making waves...

Like most men, I had big dreams of becoming an astronaut, firefighter or professional skateboarder, NOT A QUILTER. Even to this day I refer to myself as a "Textile Artist" not a quilt maker. Never in my wildest dreams did I think that I would be a part of this crazy industry, but **I LOVE IT**.

I stumbled blindly into the world of sewing and quiltmaking through my Mom's shop, "The Cotton Ball" in Morro Bay, CA. I started to work in the craft department to pick up a few extra hours a week while my wife was obtaining her teaching credentials. I stocked small bottles of paint, and learned to roll bees wax candles. I started to teach customers how to build fountains and make mosaic stepping stones. The creative energy in the shop was overwhelming, but I was not like most of the other customers.

I spent my free time surfing and skateboarding. I was also working in the restaurant industry, as I had been since my first job. I knew very little about sewing and even less about the art of quiltmaking. I had sewn, but only a few small items. Okay... garments to customize my action figures. As I set upon my quest for manhood, I progressed in developing my manly sewing skills by making the curtains for my 1971 VW Bus, and the jacket I would wear while snowboarding. These early ventures into creative and utilitarian sewing would be my roadmap into this world of quilting. In other words, I am as shocked as you are that you are reading this.

My seascape quilts were originally patterned after the paintings of **Christian Lassen** and **Robert Wyland**. I wanted to recreate their multi-perspective angles of the ocean with fabric. My approach was to vision myself snorkeling, wearing a face mask with my head just at the ocean surface. With the face mask half under the water and half above. I could see everything now! This includes the sky, deep into space and to the very bottom of the sea. Get the picture?

This study of seascape quilts and the different approaches to design and quilt architecture has led me to a fantastic career as a sewing and quilting educator, as well as being a sewing machine service technician.

I still refer to myself as a beginner quilter with a ton of practice. My work is not mind blowing by any means, but it is achievable by just about anyone who is willing to take a new approach to quiltmaking. This book not only features several of my most popular quilt patterns but also a gallery of the quilts that have joined me along this journey. I hope you enjoy them, and maybe even learn something too.

Table of Contents

Table of Contents

Rob Appell

"The Dolphin Dance"

Created in 2001, Morro Bay, CA
Finished Dimensions 50" x 84"

Supply List

1 Yard of Theme Fabric

2 Pillow Panels with at least a 10 x 10 scene (or any large print)

½ Yard of Light Fabric

½ Yards of Two Medium Fabrics

½ Yard of Dark Fabric

⅓ Yard of additional Medium Fabric for large center row

⅜ Yard of Interior Border

⅞ Yard Exterior Border

½ Yard of Binding Fabric

Dolphin Dance is the first quilt I had ever written a pattern for; do not worry, it has been edited and proofed to death, it should be just about right now.

The quilt started one night when my wife had gone off to her dance class and I had convinced myself to attempt a quilt. I had limited experience with a rotary cutter and mat, so I began to strip-piece the layout for the top of the quilt. I was not pleased with the linear layout of the project. Out of frustration I began to cut the strips in the opposite direction to the construction. I cut different sized pieces and "scrambled" them into position. I needed to play with the offset layout of the pillow panel rows so I shifted the wide, dark fabric in the "strip set rows" and the quilt came to life.

After years of teaching this quilt and selling patterns nationally, I can still hardly believe the success of this simple quilt. I have had students make this project in a variety of different themed fabrics such as clocks, coffee, Asian, jungle and cats - just to name a few.

The project works great with any theme fabric and is great starting place for any quilter.

Step 1

Choose ½ yard cuts of four different fabrics. One light, two mediums, and a dark. First using the light and two mediums, fold the ½ yards from selvage to selvage. This should give you pieces that are folded 18"x 22½". With a rotary cutter working parallel to the 22½" side, trim away your raw edge. Now cut two strips each, 2½" x 45" and 4½" x 45". Also Cut one additional 1½ " strip of your light fabric, set aside for later use.

Step 2

Prepare to create three separate strip set rows, each measuring 12 ½" x 45"when sewn together. Choose different combinations of the light and two medium fabrics. Be aware of the direction of print on your fabric. Sew the 45" strips together in an alternating fashion. Start with a 4½" strip, then a 2½" strip, and then repeat. Each "strip set" row will have four strips in it. Use the same fabric in both 2½" strips per strip set. Make sure to use a different fabric for the top 4 ½ "strip each time. This will create a balanced look.

Step 3 Cut each of the three strip sets parallel to the 12½" side. Cut one 11 ½" strip, two 5½" strips, and two 2½" strips. Save excess fabric, can be used to increase the size of the interior of the quilt top, or pieced into a strip for the additional yardage needed on the back.

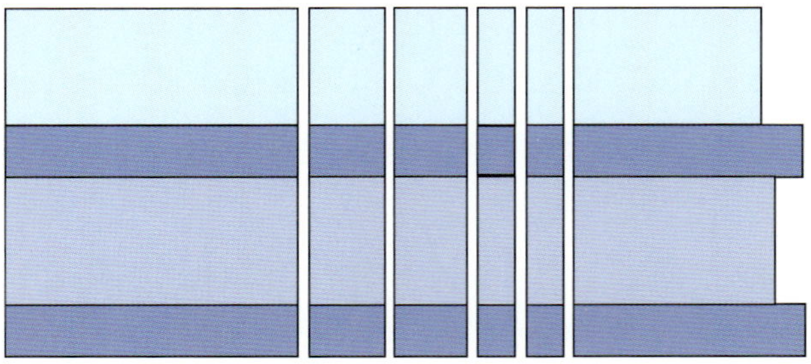

Step 4

Take your fourth fabric, the dark. Cut a strip 12½" x 45" (set the remainder aside). Now cutting parallel to the 12 ½" side, trim your edge, and cut three 5½" strips, six 2½" strips, and six 1½" strips. This will leave a little extra behind for error.

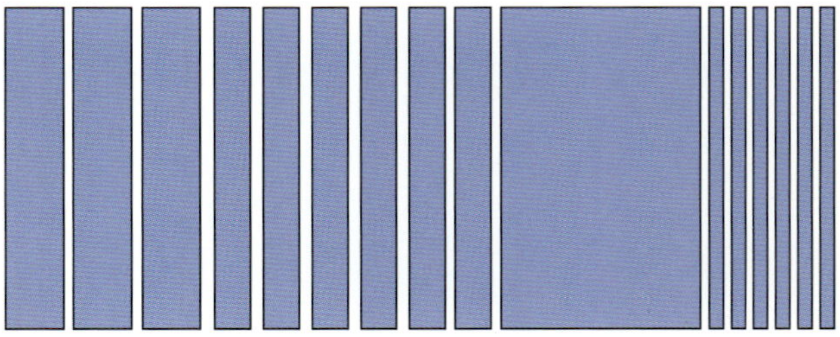

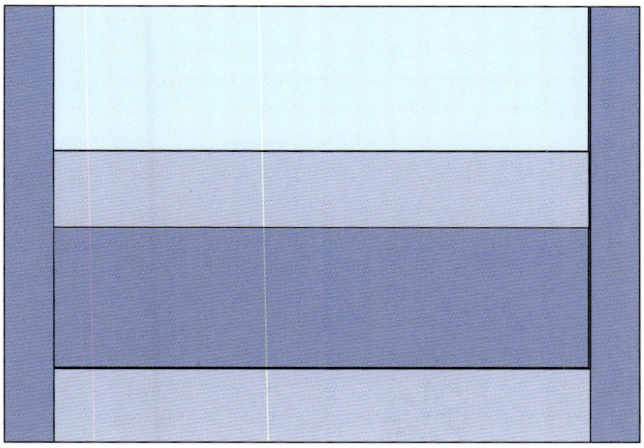

Step 5

Now begin to create the "strip pieced" rows. It is recommend to do the layout for all three "strip pieced" rows prior to sewing any of the rows together, this allows for variations based on the way the colors are working together. Take one of your 11½" strips and sew a 1½" dark strip to either side. Measurements in example are finished measurements with ¼" seam allowance. Do this step to all three 11½" strips.

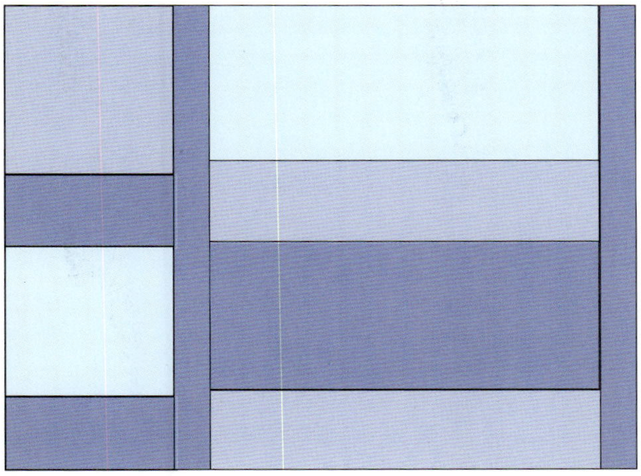

Step 6

Choose two 5½" pieced strips that are the same. Place one of these strips on each side of the 11½" block. (These strips should be different than the 11½" block.) From here use different combinations of the 5½" strips and 2½" Strips. One 5½" dark strip per "strip set" row (the placement of this strip varies, please see the layout for the rows before assembling), and two 2½" dark strips, one on each end to finish the "strip set" rows. Please see the diagram on the last page for complete layout. Again, it is recommended to do the whole layout prior to sewing. Each Strip Set Row should finish at 36".

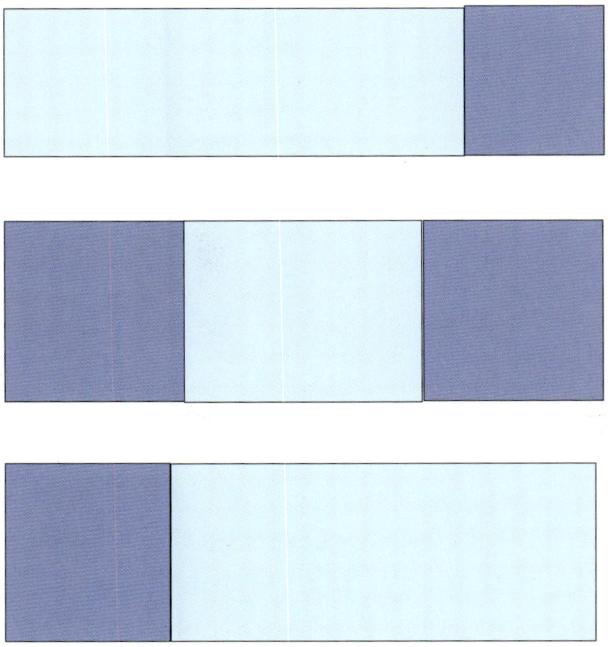

Step 7

Begin to create the basic rows. These rows will use three new fabrics. The theme fabric (A), the pillow panel (B), and a coordinating print (C). Cut your pillow panels to the desired size, in this pattern they are 10" squares. By cutting the panels first, you can make size adjustments to the width of your cuts to fabrics A and C. The motif of the pillow panel may also determine it's placement in the basic rows. Cut fabrics A and C into strips 45" x the panel width. Sew three Basic rows, A to B, C to A to C, and B to A.

Basic Layout for Quilt Top

1″ strip of light fabric.

Row using Pillow Panel and Theme Fabric.

Strip Set Row 1. Choose a Strip Set Row that has light fabrics in the upper left hand corner.

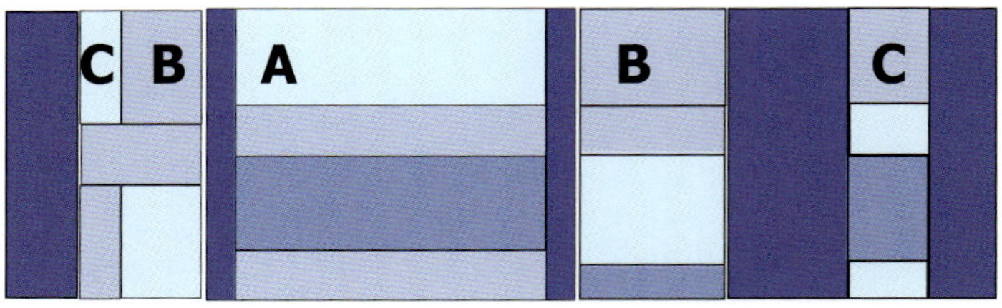

Row using the Theme Fabric in the center and medium fabrics on either side. I used a fabric not found any where else in the quilt to add variety.

Strip Set Row. Notice the center block is shifted by using the 5″ dark strip on the left side of the center block.

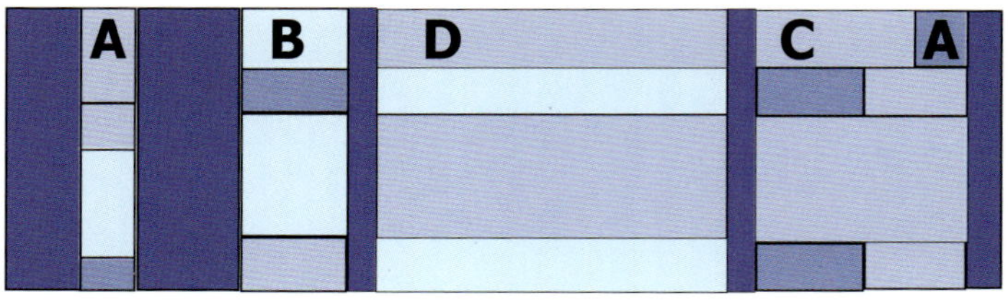

Row using Pillow Panel and Theme Fabric.

Strip Set Row with the same configuration as the first one used.

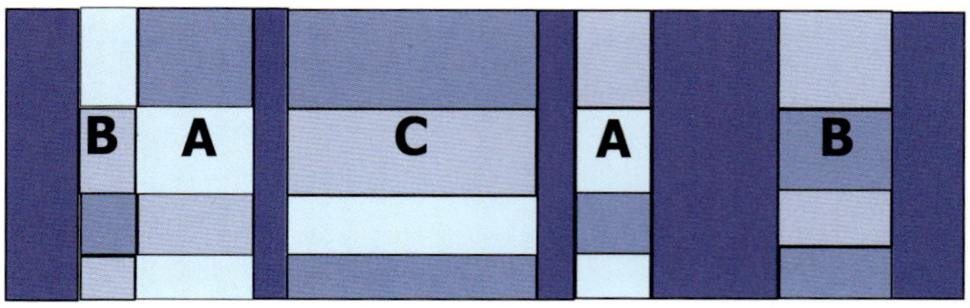

3″ Row using border from Pillow Panel. Or 4″ Dark Fabric Strip set aside from Step #4

Interior Border is cut at 2 inches. Exterior border is cut at 5 inches. (Borders Not Shown)

The letters A, B, and C, correspond to entire Strip Set Rows. By following this format, the quilt sets up for a beautiful scramble of strip set row pieces with no overlap of color.

Student Quilts....

A Double "Dolphin Dance" by Chris; not to shabby for this guy's first quilt!

Gigi's advanced version of The "Dolphin Dance" with some great paper pieced dolphins.

Linda spiced up the border on her "Dolphin Dance" quilt with some "piano keys."

The Man - The Machine - The Motion

People seem to make a big deal about my free-motion machine quilting, and I was not too sure why until recently. You see, I feel that my stitch quality is average and I really do not do anything fancy, but I do quilt fast. I found out that the lack of superb quality in the machine quilting made people feel like they too could one day be bold enough to show off their own work. (Heck, if Rob can get away with it so can we). Well I am just fine with that. I would rather encourage people due to my imperfections, than to scare them off because I too was perfect, like the rest of the quilt police.

So if I feel that my free-motion work is so average, why did I decide to waste this page to write about it? Simple, I have been told that the way I quilt my scenes brings life into them. Plus, I love to free-motion quilt, so, good or not, here is my recipe for success.

The Man – or Woman (in most cases). This refers to your attitude and mind set. Personally, I find the more relaxed my body is and the better clarity of mind set, the more comfortably, the more freely the more fluidly, I can quilt. Ok, enough psycho babble, have a glass of wine, put on your favorite music (headphones are nice to really be able to tune out the rest of life while quilting) and get your body comfortable. Elbows down, hands flat, fingers spread and thumbs almost touching. Sit up straight, and do not kink your neck to see the stitching. Believe me, if you can see the stitches falling one after another you are moving way too slow.

The Machine – Yes, I have my Pfavorite Pfaff Pfor quilting, but I am not here to sell machines, please come to my store for that. So what do you need? Space and speed make every machine quilter's set-up so much more enjoyable. My machine is not set into a frame, but does feature over nine inches of head space, or the distance from the needle to the body of the machine. It is also nice and tall, seven inches of opening from top to bottom, and this helps if I need to roll my quilt up to get a big half under the head of the machine. It is set into a table so that the needle plate is level with the surface of the table. I use a "Sew Slip" brand glide mat made of Teflon on the bed of my machine. Ok, try to follow along, this mat fits over the feed dogs and under the quilt, it is Teflon, so now you have no drag on the quilt, and you can quilt super fast with less fatigue. Lastly, I slide on the "Machingers" brand gloves and now I have Spiderman finger tips, no not webs, just super traction. This allows for superior control. Yes, I do look silly in them, but it is worth it.

The Motion – This is the hard one to describe. I could say "just do it" and to some I do. For the rest of us, the words of advice come from a good friend of mine "find your happy place". Rhythm is the key, being able to keep the machine running at a constant pace so that you have regular stitch length. For some it is faster than for others, but I do strongly believe that the faster you are able to run the machine, the smoother the motion of the quilt is under the needle. Most of us struggle with inconsistent stitches, so find the link between the machine's speed and your hand motion. Remember that not all quilting styles will be performed at the same pace.

If you have big stitches, then speed up your machine and/or slow down your hands. In contrast, if you have small stitches, then speed up your hands or cool it on the gas of the machine. Corners are tough, so slow down the machine as you approach, and speed up as you whip out of the corners like a Porsche on the Autobahn. Last but not least, stop thinking about it all so much, take a deep breath, drop your shoulders and try to let the fabrics and threads speak to each other as you hang on for the ride. Remember every quilt is simply practice for that one great one.

"One Cool Fish"

Named for the Angel Fish on the bottom right with her free motion machine embroidered sunglasses.

This was done to prevent the use of a seam ripper when I got a bit too wild with the machine quilting.

Created in 2002, Morro Bay, CA
Finished Dimensions 45″ x 65″

Painted And Fused

These quilts were a blast to create. I not only was able to bring my love for the airbrush to the textile world, but by using a large piece of "fabric" for the center medallion, I was able to design these quilt tops in a flash. I painted these center panels myself using an airbrush and thinned down water-based acrylic paint. I did use a textile medium to make the fabric washable, but if you have ever gotten water-based acrylic paint on you clothes, and let it dry, you may have found it did not wash out even without adding the textile medium. You may also be challenged as a painter, so the use of a large fabric panel that you can purchase at fine quilt shops (like my Mom's), can work equally well.

A quick run down of the quilts...

Using the center panel, I created a pseudo quilt sandwich (look it up) by layering the back ground of the quilt top, a layer of batting, and the center panel. Keep in mind the background to the quilt top is considerably larger than the center panel. Then, with a straight stitch, I used my sewing machine to sew around the "peanut" shape of the panels I was using. If your panel is not in the shape of a peanut, sew around it with a soft curving line. If it were going to be a straight sewn line, you may as well piece it into place. Once the edges of the panel are sewn down, I very carefully cut away the rest of the panel and batting to the sewn line. This will now form a canvas for appliqué that will have extra batting in the center of the quilt so that you may achieve that 'Trapunto' effect.

Now that your canvas is set up, you will want to hide those raw edges of the batting and panel with appliqués. You know the drill, no more duct tape, just fusible web, iron and scissors. You will find this approach better described on page 16. Once all of your appliqué work is completed you should have what appears to be a porthole view into paradise. It should look as if your perspective is the same as that lion hiding in the jungle looking out of the foliage into a beautiful picturesque scene.

"Blooming Paradise"

Created in 2005, Morro Bay, CA
Finished Dimensions 42"x 60"

"Ever Feel Small?"

Created in 2004, Morro Bay, CA
Finished Dimensions 40" x 50"

Under Watercolor Quilts

"Ever Feel Small" is my third watercolor quilt and the story is a lifelong lesson... 7 a.m. at Willow Creek, Big Sur, California. Swell was a mixed northwest about twelve foot at sixteen second intervals. No wind, a clear sky, in other words; a surfer's dream come true. Randy, a friend who had moved to Monterey from Morro Bay, and I were the only two guys in the line up that morning. Randy had picked the spot as it was half way between each of our homes. Willow Creek was new to me, the waves were bigger than I am used to surfing and the waves were coming fast, and from deep water. The approach was all large boulders and giant kelp, so paddling out to the surfline was not an easy task.

I get a bit nervous in new situations, but I was jumping for big surf. I made the paddle out okay. A few deep duck dives, but I survived, until the first real thumper of a wave rolled through. I turned and tried to paddle into the beast, but it simply tossed me down head first and held me underwater like a rag doll. Keep in mind, I have been through this all before, many times... just never at Willow Creek. I found the surface with a gulp of air that stank of panic but nevertheless, jumped back on my board. I had to get back outside of the set waves before the ocean truly showed me its awesome power.

I was a not too excited to find myself far from shore with the only way back to the beach to ride the waves that just nearly drowned me. Another wave was on its way and Randy mentioned that it was mine. Even though I was sure he was wrong, once again I started working to catch the wave. This time no disaster, as a matter of fact I made the drop down the face of the wave and proceeded to surf it with style. Boy, what a feeling! I only caught a few more waves before I safely beached myself like the little rag doll I had been that morning.

I drove home in silence, but thought less of myself for letting the fear of the waves ruin a perfect surfing day. As I began to digest what had happened that morning I realized that I was perfectly capable of surfing the waves that day, and I had let my anxiety get the best of me. My fears had stifled my dreams. I came home and started this quilt.

Notice the two little surfers on the left hand side. They represent Randy and myself on that big day that left me feeling rather small. I have surfed Willow Creek many times since, and always get a bit thrashed, but I also always get one good wave. The lesson is, do not let your fear of the unknown or failure prevent you from doing your best. When you catch that perfect wave, ride it and rejoice that you did something that not everyone can do.

Now take this to your sewing room, and try that project or technique you have always wanted to do. Do not worry about the wipe-out or use of the seam ripper. Try it, and take pride in the fact that you have now stepped out of your box.

This pattern will focus on the creation of a watercolor style background in the theme of the coral reefs. We will then have the option of appliqué and/or trapunto work on top of our background. For your first project I recommend using 2″ fusible grid interfacing as your base. As you become more advanced you may choose to get smaller grid, or turn your squares on point for the "impressionism" style of watercolor quilts.

To determine how much grid is needed, figure the desired finished size of the quilt.

Subtract the size of the borders from the length and width of the desired size of the finished quilt.

Divide the length by 1.5.

Divide the width by 1.5.

Now this will tell you how many squares in the grid you need for the length and width of the finished quilts before you add the borders back on.

If the number has a remainder, either round the number of squares needed up or down. Multiply the number of squares needed by the size of your grid squares; you now have a linear yardage amount. It is often necessary to piece our fusible grid interfacing to accommodate the desired quilt size.

(If using other than 2″ grid, divide the quilt size by the size of the finished block size. 2″ = 1.5, 1.5″ = 1, and so on)

Getting Started

1. If possible hang your fusible grid interfacing so that you may observe it from several feet back.
2. Pre-cut many fabrics into enough 2″ squares. Keep your fabric squares in stacks. Keep the stacks in fabric family groups. Example, skies – corals – waters – etc.

Please follow the diagrams on the next pages for step-by-step layout. Place your fabrics right side up on the fusible side of the grid.

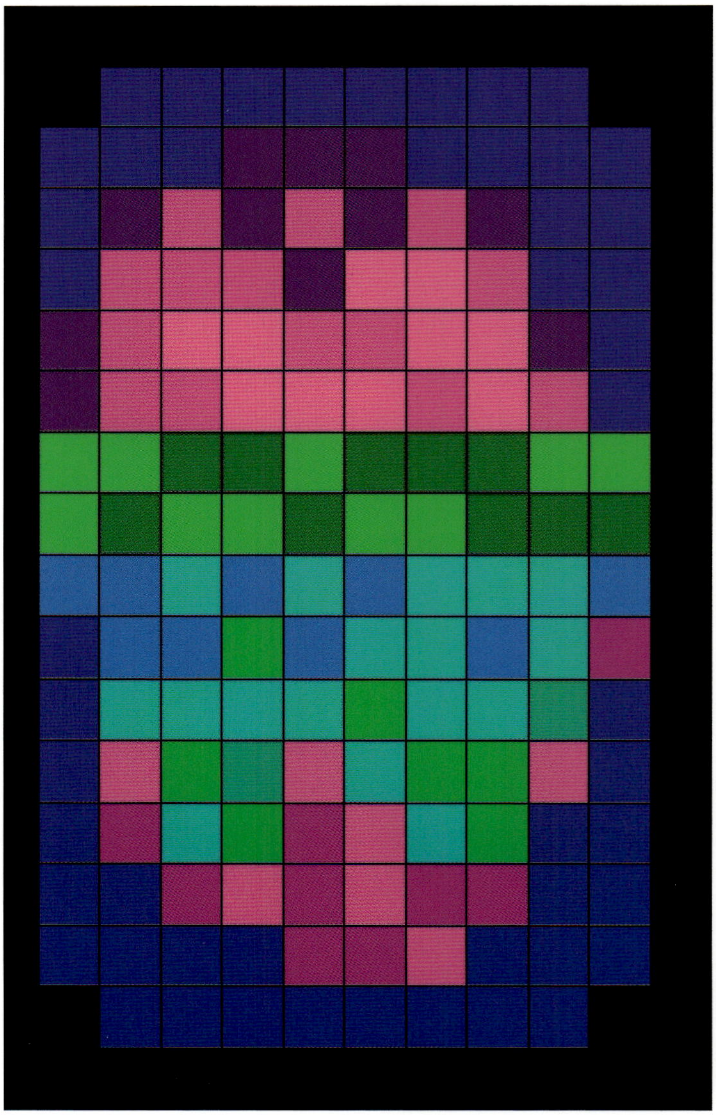

Once you are pleased with your background, fuse your fabrics to the grid. Please follow the directions provided with the grid for accurate fusing and sewing.

I love to appliqué on top of my watercolor backgrounds. Take this opportunity to make the quilt fantastic. Create your own paradise and invite all our undersea friends to live in your Under Watercolor.

Placement

Start as if you were building a jigsaw puzzle. Build your perimeter edge first. Simply count out the amount of squares needed, mark each corner, and start building your outer edge. Determine the line for the Horizon. Not the center of the quilt, somewhere in the upper third.

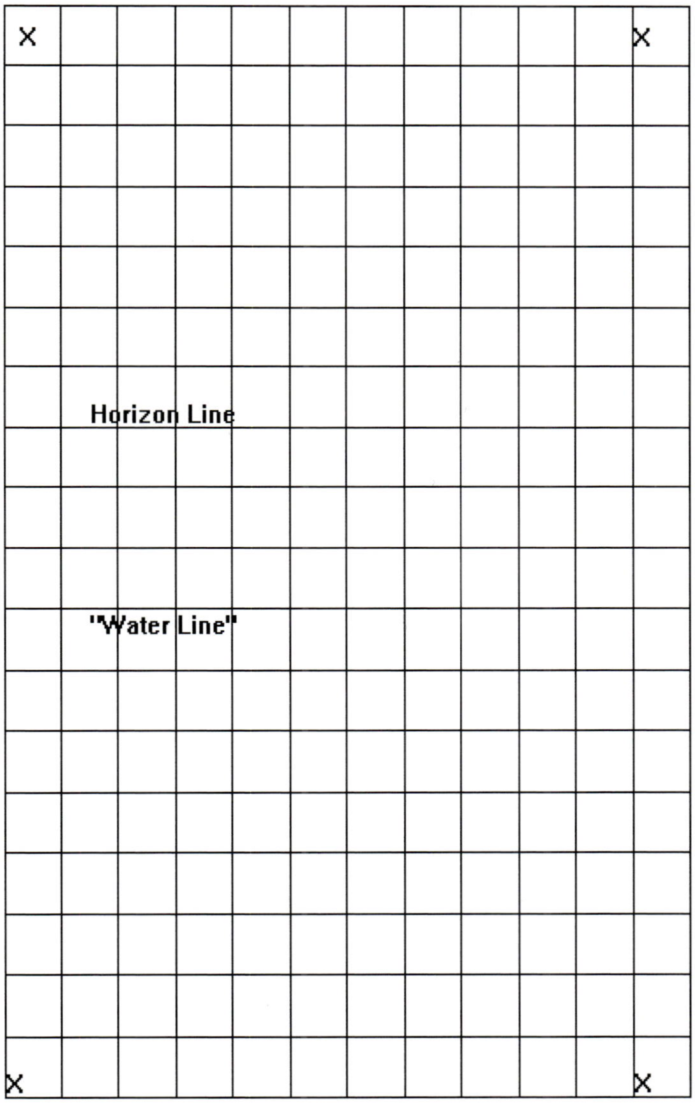

Next, determine the "water line" this is the division between the water surface, and the underwater portion of the quilt. Not in The center, somewhere in the lower third of the quilt.

Starting with your darkest space/sky. Your placement does not need to be perfectly symmetrical.

Next are the fabrics for the area between the "water line" and the Horizon.

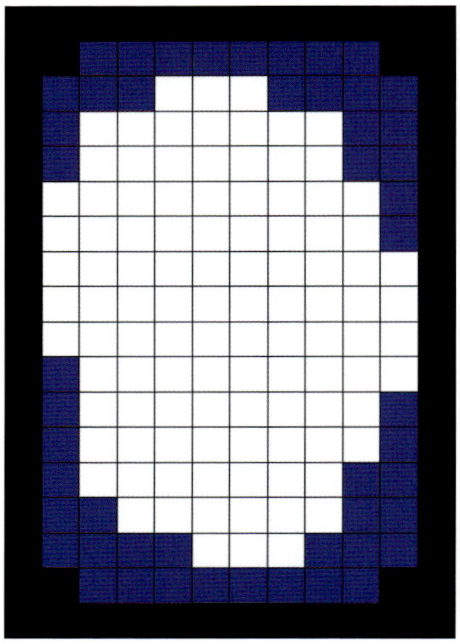

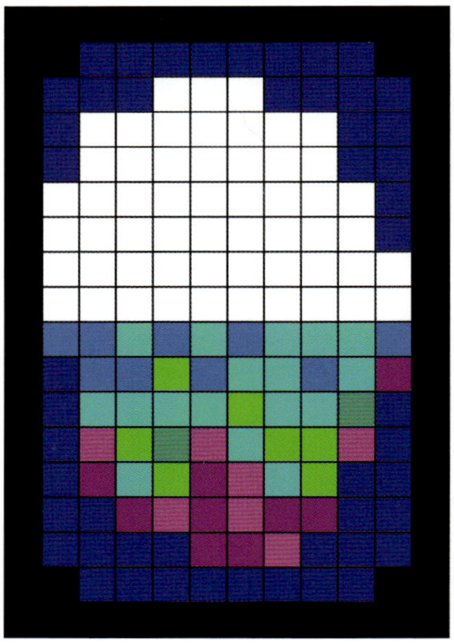

Now add the fabrics for below the "water line" I find addressing the quilt in sections helps control the placement of fabrics, and expedites the process, so the quilt does not seem so overwhelming.

Finally, fill the area of the sky. You may find that you have created a light source such as the sun or moon. If necessary adjust the surface water fabrics to allow for the reflection.

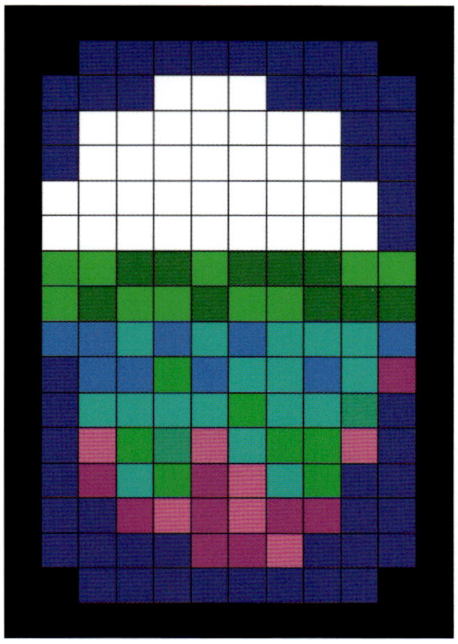

No More Duct Tape

If it was not for fusible web, I most likely would never have become a quilt artist. I find that the appliqué process is what really excites me about the design phase of each quilt that I do. Do not get me wrong, the Free Motion Machine Quilting is still my favorite part of each quilt, but it is the placement and approach to the appliqué that lend to the machine quilting. So here is how it is done.

Fusible appliqué, AKA Raw Edge Appliqué, is done by using a fusible web on the back side of the appliqué to be fabric. So what is this fusible web stuff? Basically, there are several brands of fusible web, but I do prefer Heat-n-Bond Lite by ThermOweb™. Fusible web is a layer of light weight fabric glue set on a sheet of paper in a web format, and usually sold by the yard. When handling the key is to **remember, the rough side is the glue side**. My students chant this mantra three times before being allowed to approach their ironing surface.

To protect your iron and ironing surface you must only allow the glue to come in contact with the things you want stuck together. Sounds simple enough, the Heat & Bond is heat activated. You may handle it, trace on it, pre-cut it all day long, but never touch it with an iron until you are sure. Of course follow the manufacturer's direction for use but here are a few key steps.

☯ Always make sure there is at least a quarter of an inch of fabric showing all the way around from the fusible web. It is always a good idea to put a Teflon pressing sheet down under the fabrics or a scrap of old cloth to also help protect your ironing surface.

☯ Only place the hot iron on the paper (smooth) side of the fusible web. IronOff brand hot iron cleaner, will save your iron if you forget, but nothing will save your ironing surface.

☯ If tracing a pattern, make sure your design is Transposed (reversed) from the original.

☯ Never pre-cut the appliqués, as you want the glue to come completely to the edge of each appliqué to act as a fray blocker. This will help prevent the fabric from fraying over time and minimizes the need for sewing machine accuracy later.

☯ If using a batik fabric, do not over iron. Batik fabric has no sizing so it will soak up the glue web faster making it harder for the glue to stick to the background that the appliqué is set upon.

☯ Leave the paper on the back side of the appliqué until you are sure you do not need to fine tune your cutting. The paper helps stabilize the fabric for fine cutting.

"Watercolor Whales"

My first watercolor quilt and last waved edge quilt.

Created in 2002, Morro Bay, CA
Finished Dimensions 39" x 39"

"Waves and Whales"

This quilt was created for my Gallery showing with artist Dale Evers.
This is a 2 inch square watercolor technique with fusible applique.

Created in 2004, Morro Bay, CA
Finished Dimensions 42" x 50"

"Moonlight Migration"

This quilt now hangs on the wall of my Ocean Knowledge Mentor.
Constructed using the Quick Fuse Seascape technique.

Created in 2004, Morro Bay, CA
Finished Dimensions 45" x 60"

"The Parrot on the Point"

The Original "Quick Fuse Seascape" Quilt

Created in 2001, Morro Bay, CA
Finished Dimensions 42" x 55"

"Another Perfect Day"

Purchased by Dale Evers for
The Nature Quest Gallery

Created in 2004, Morro Bay, CA
Finished Dimensions 60" x 60"

"King of the Jungle
King of the Reef"

Quick Fuse Seascape technique

Commissioned 2006, Oregon
Finished Dimensions 50" x 45"

"Tranquito Sunrise"

Spanglish for Tranquil Sunrise
Quick Fuse Seascape technique
and cover shot on pattern.

Created in 2003, Morro Bay, CA
Finished Dimensions 40" x 45"

"Tag... You're It!"

This quilt was named for the large blue school of fish chasing the one Great White Shark

Created in 2004, Morro Bay, CA
Finished Dimensions 42"x 45"

"Sea Frolic II"

Quilt created for Michael Miller Fabrics to promote the new line of fabric

Created in 2004, Morro Bay, CA
Finished Dimensions 45" x 60"

Quick Fuse Seascape Quilts

"Quick Fuse" Seascape Quilts are my favorite! So fast, fun and easy. This pattern will teach you a method that will hopefully be used in many of your fantastic quilts still to be created. The basis for these projects is creating a simple, yet dramatic background on which to appliqué. This technique does not use muslin for our base to build upon. A few simple strips of fabric sewn together will save hours of time. In fact, I personally find the faster I work in making fabric choices for my background, the better the quilt. If you grab fabrics that visually work together and represent each section of the desired seascape, there will be no time to second-guess yourself. An artistic moment is born. Rely on your instinct; if it is ugly when you finish give it away for Christmas.

To get started we must understand a few terms used in this pattern. I like to create quilts that give a tropical feel and span from the Galaxies above to the bottom of the ocean. This does not mean that you must have planets and sea snails together in all your quilts, but try to build a background that reaches out from your comfort zone. The background seen in the reference diagram has sky, water and substrate (the bottom of the sea).

Term 1 The Horizon Line divides the ocean surface from the sky. The horizon is never in the middle of the quilt.

Term 2 The Water Line divides the ocean surface from the underwater. The Water Line is never in the middle of the quilt.

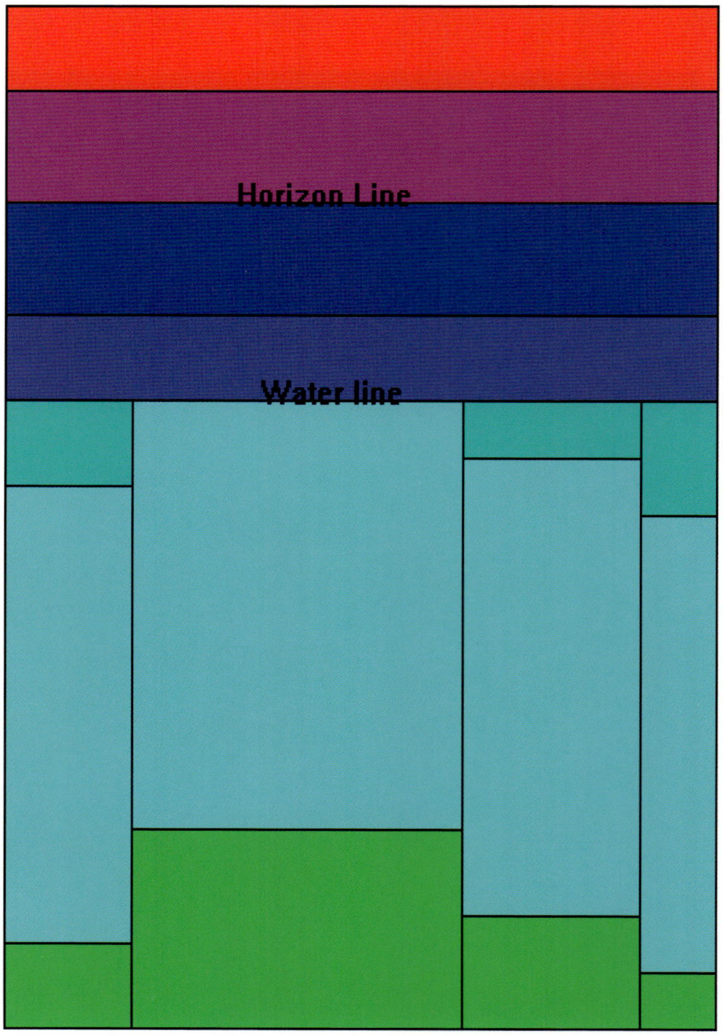

Easy rules to follow? Yes! Once you have mastered the simple layout for backgrounds, get creative. Eliminate the sky, or play with the perspective. The perspective is what builds the depth to the quilt. Use the amount of water surface to build that perspective. The greater the water surface is, the larger your island (if there is an island in your paradise) becomes. The smaller the water surface, the bigger the fish can be, the higher the dolphins can jump.

Do not neglect your sky. Create incredible sunsets, flocks of birds, or even the full moon and its glow. Islands should reach up past the Horizon Line and into the sky. Leaping dolphins should do the same. The sun can be down behind the Horizon Line or up high in the sky.

Never place a sun or moon in the middle of your sky, keep it at least slightly offset. The sun or moon is the light source, so practice proper ***Illumination***. This gives perfect perspective.

Recommended Supplies for a Simple Seascape

- ¼ Yard each of two different 'Sky' fabrics
- ⅜ Yard each of two different 'Water' fabrics for the Surface Water
- ½ Yard each of two or three different 'Underwater' fabrics
- ¼ Yard each of two different 'Bottom' fabrics

Applique fabrics that fit the Background Fabrics above

Step 1 Sew the fabrics for the underwater together. Please note: I do not supply measurements for cutting. Let the design of the fabric be your guide.

Step 2 Cut the sewn fabrics into vertical strips. Cut at least four vertical strips. Use width measurements that are visually proportionate.

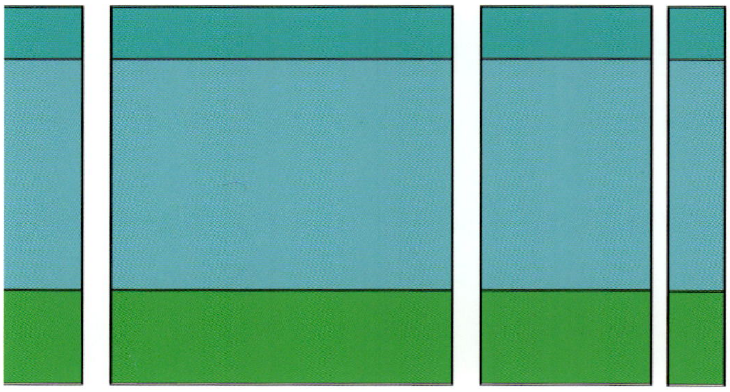

Step 3 Sew the vertical strips back together in a stair step fashion. Keep your largest strip in the center and randomly place the other strips on both sides of the center strip. This is the time to adjust fabrics to keep with the light source.

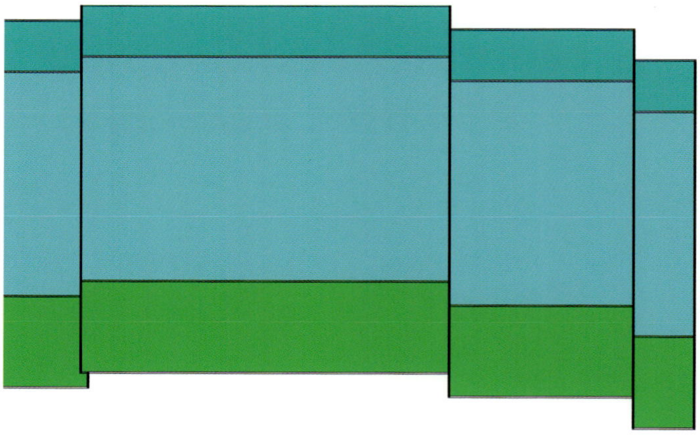

Step 4 Finally, we true up our underwater.

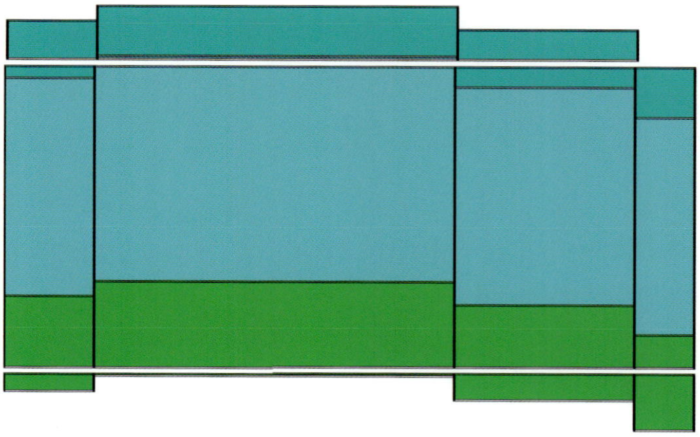

Step 5 Prepare the fabrics for above the water line. Simply sew your fabric strips together. (2A) Create the water surface. Work up from the water line. Your water fabrics should get darker in color as they transition from the water line to the horizon line (darkest color at the horizon).

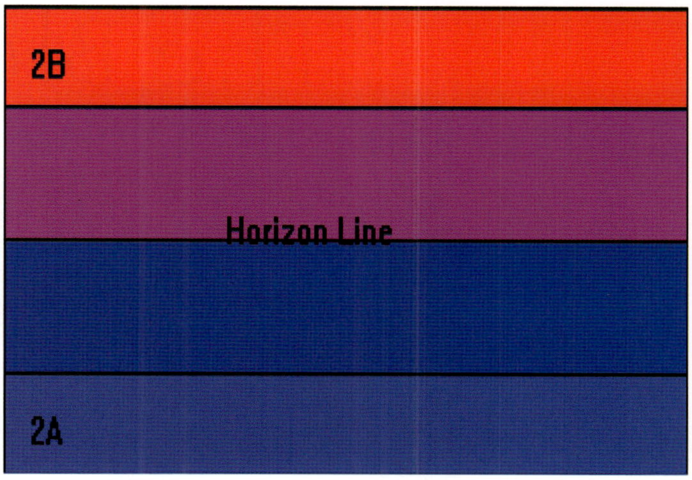

Create the sky. The sky's color variations are endless. For a blue sky, colors will darken as they approach the heavens. For a sunset, your colors can change in either direction. If the sun is still high in the sky, use a purple or fuchsia at the horizon. If the sun has just set, use yellow or orange at the horizon.

Caution: Try to keep your scene in proportion. Sizes will vary, just be aware of location, theme and color of each object.

Step 6 Sew together the Underwater fabric set and the above the water line fabric set. This seam will become the water line.

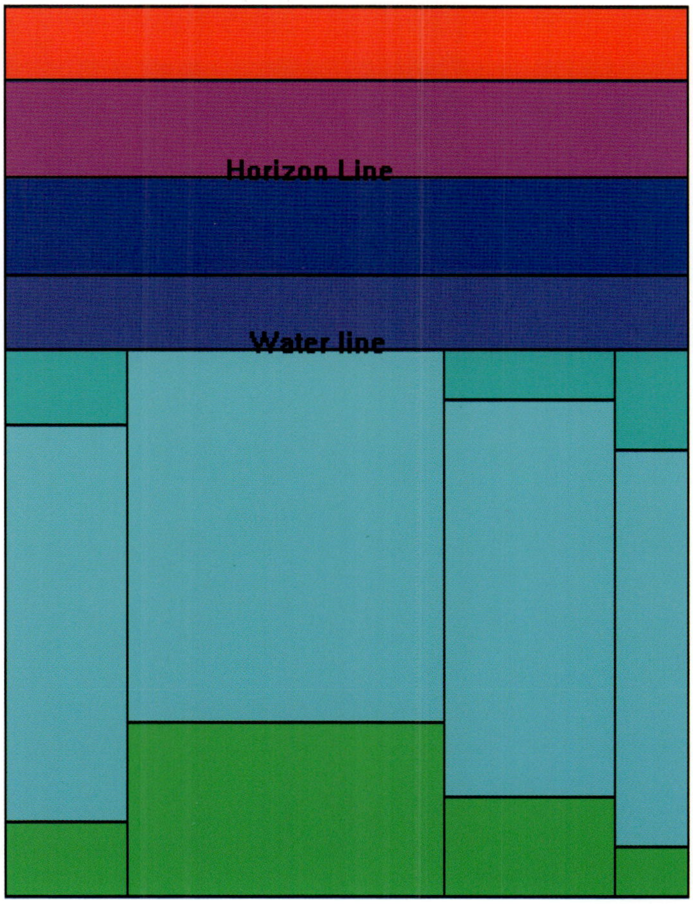

Step 7 Prepare for the appliqués.

This is when the fun starts. I prefer to use fusible web for my appliqués, then anchor them in the machine quilting process. I prefer "Heat-n-Bond Lite" for my fusible web. I will often apply a large piece on the back of a fabric that has a lot of items, for my appliqué. If I do not use every object I simply save it for my next quilt. Try to create an environment that will achieve two goals. First, hide the seams. Be creative with your placement to help the seams blend into the background. Second, use the appliques to blend the colors while telling a story.

Create your own paradise!

"The Blue Crew"

Created in 2007, Morro Bay, CA
Finished Dimensions 45"x 60"

Quick Fuse Seascape Quilts Part Two

This diagram is useful when blending an assortment of fabrics that are basically solid looking prints. I use this format when I cannot find an allover busy reef scenic fabric to use as my base for the underwater. I will need more fabrics for appliqué to bring the scene to life, but this is a great option when large scale allover prints are not available.

I then start my appliqué process by forming the sea mounts, or the base of the islands that are underwater. This "underwater land form" is the area from which the corals grow. The corals are home to the small fish and so on. The surface water usually has an island on it that connects the underwater land form to the surface. Please see the quilt below to get a better idea for your appliqué.

BLUE CREW SUPPLY LIST FOR BACKGROUND

** Does not include Applique fabrics.*

¼ Yard 'Sky' fabric

½ Yard basic print for 'Surface of Water'

¾ Yard variegated or batik fabric for 'Underwater'

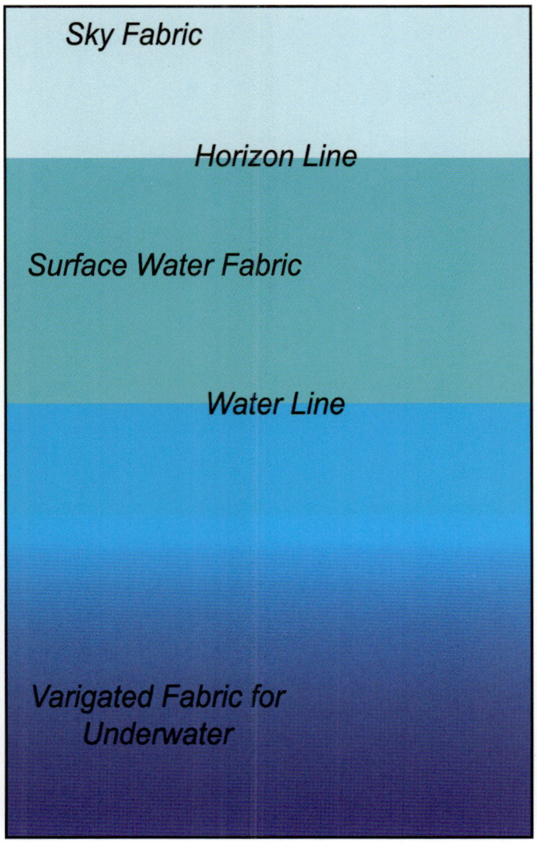

Keep in mind; most of the detail will come from the applique work, so it is cool to let the backgrounds be very subtle.

"Scuba Time"

What a pleasure it is to get that box of goodies from Michael Miller Fabrics and the only requirements are ... "use these fabrics to make us a quilt."

Created in 2008, Morro Bay, CA
Finished Dimensions 45"x 60"

Here are a few simple steps to follow to create your own paradise using this awesome technique. First build your background canvas from a repeat of the Scuba Time print, a few pieces of Krystal, the Peaceful Water and Clouds. Please note that the measurements seen in the diagram to the left can be flexible to help your quilt fit your needs.

36″ x 6″ 36″ x 29″ 36″ x 8″

After applying fusible web to the backside of all of your appliqué fabrics, start by cutting large sections from the waterfall fabrics. Once the falls are created you will know how to position the underwater rocks and corals to help fill in the reef. Try to use the appliqués to hide the seams in your background as well as balance the colors in your project.

Finish your quilt by filling in the spaces underwater with more cuttings from the additional panels of Scuba Time for the scene. Create islands from scraps from the waterfall fabrics. Place highlights on the water using a variety of shades of Fairy Frost, then apply your borders, sandwich and quilt. Make sure to anchor your appliqués down with your free-motion quilting machine.

Ways To Create The Appliqué

As I mentioned previously I love to create appliqués using the "Raw Edge" method, also known as fusible appliqués. Each quilt may have a need for a variety of styles of fusible appliqués based on the background fabrics as well as the fabrics you have chosen to work with. There really is no correct approach, but here are the three major ways to create fusible appliqués.

Patterns – in this process, you will have a line drawing of a pattern piece to be set as a fusible appliqué. Make sure that the pattern is transposed (a horizontal mirror image of the original). Using a fine pen or pencil, trace the pattern piece onto the smooth side of the fusible web. I prefer to trace to the outside of the pattern's line to slightly enlarge my appliqué, I then also cut to the outside of the line as well, this usually creates about a sixteenth of an inch larger appliqué than the pattern which can be useful in overlapping the appliqués slightly if you are creating multiple pieces of appliqué into one pattern, a dogs face for example will feature several individual pieces traced and cut from separate fabrics to create the dog.

Fussy Cut Appliques - The most simple of the processes to describe. Find a fabric that contains an image that you want to use as an appliqué, place a chunk of fusible web on the back side of the fabric. Make sure that your chunk of web is larger than the fussy cut appliqué to be. Set the web with an iron, and then simply cut out the appliqué on the line seen in the fabric. For example, an all over fish print fabric will have several potential appliqués, but let's say you just want that one lion fish - this process will allow you to capture just one creature. Granted, the rest of the fish nearby may be sacrificed in the process, but at least you have one great appliqué.

Free Cut Appliqués – Mostly used when there is nothing else better I can do. Meaning, I want to make some rocks for one of my reef scenes. I need a large, relatively neutral looking piece to plant corals on and have fish swim through. So I place a large piece of fusible on the back of the fabric to be used, usually batik in this type of work, set with an iron and let cool. I then just let my scissors do the work; I randomly cut the shapes to create the things I need for the scene. These appliqués are usually dressed up with fussy cut pieces on top or the machine quilting process itself..

How to quilt them down -
Now the real fun begins. Once the entire scene is perfect in my eyes, I will go back through all of the appliqués and remove the paper, and fine tune the placement of each appliqué. I then press down all of the appliqués at once. I do NOT use gliding motions with the iron; I lift and press, lift

and press. If you slide the iron, you will most likely fold an appliqué in half and melt it to the bottom of the iron. Once the appliqués are all pressed, I have a quilt top to sandwich. I safety-pin baste my sandwich then get right to the Free Motion Machine quilting process.

Most folks prefer to satin stitch the edges of their appliqués. I only use this technique for appliqués that will be machine washed and dried. The satin stitching helps prevent the edges from fraying in the wash. My quilts hang on the wall, so I just hit the appliqués with thread.

Well, I do not really hit them; I dress them up and permanently attach them to the quilt in the same step. I do start the Machine Quilting from the center of the quilt and work out in all directions, but my focus is stitching around all of the appliqués first. I am doing free motion quilting so the feed dogs are down and I use the free-motion foot so I can move the quilt under the machine's needle however I please. The look will be of a straight stitch that follows the outline of the entire appliqué. When the quilt is viewed from the back, you can usually recognize all of the appliqués as outlined.

Trouble shooting for Machine Quilting With Fusible Appliqué-
The fusible web can be a bit hard to quilt through, so try not to overdo the layering of appliqués. Usually two to three layers is all most machines can handle. If you are skipping stitches, slow your movement down. The fusible web can slightly alter the loop formed by the needle and miss in your bobbin case. If your thread frays, clean off the glue from the back of the needle and always use good quality thread. If the thread breaks more than once in a few stitches replace the needle, it is worn out. You can expect to go through two or three needles in a wall quilt. Don't sweat it; needles are cheaper than a therapist.

"Beyond The Tides"

My trophy quilt as seen on 'Simply Quilts' Landscape Challenge, Episode 1131.
Quick Fuse Seascape technique.

Created in 2005, Morro Bay, CA
Finished Dimensions 50" x 72"

Lights... Camera....Action!

Alex Anderson calms my nerves seconds before "Action" on the set of Simply Quilts at the Weller/Grossman Studios, Burbank California

As seen on **HGTV's Simply Quilts**
The Story: For a few years it was apparent to me that getting on Simply Quilts was big time. I am not much of a TV watcher, but was aware of the impact Alex Anderson, the hostess, was having on the quilting industry. I had met her a few times at International Quilt Market, and really wanted to land the TV gig.

I found a brief moment that Alex was left unattended traveling from one show booth to another. This was my golden opportunity. As she passed I stuck out my leg and tripped her. Being the Gentleman, as I offered to help her up I handed her my Business card, and bio. I explained to her that we shared a mutual friend and that she needed me on the show.

She asked what I did, and I just happened to have a sell sheet with me that featured some of my quilts. I showed her the shots and told her I was the "king" of fusible appliqué landscapes. She replied "If I have to sit through another fusible web segment I will vomit." I asked if that was a "good" thing. She laughed. I believe it was that moment that we realized it could be a good thing, a fusible web demo, not vomiting. but we would both needed to be flexible in our approach.

She encouraged me to submit a proposal stating a few key things: Young Male, outside of the box, and willing to participate in the Quilt Challenge for the show. I was unclear as to what the challenge was, but Alex said, "Just write those words". Just a few days before the proposal was due, my email was hit with the "bomb". It was the production team for Simply Quilts, and apparently, Alex got their attention before I did. They were interested in my work. Yippee!

I was given a contract to sign stating that the Challenge show, episode 1131, was to tape in January 2005 and air late that fall. At that time I had no idea it was the final season for Simply Quilts to tape new material. The rules were few. We would have thirty days from the time that we received our photographs via email until the day we were to tape our segments in Burbank, California. The Photo was to act as our inspiration and there were no size or style limitations. Keep in mind, we had to make one completed quilt, and several step by step portions to show off our techniques.

I felt that the Photo was hand picked by Alex to help me succeed, so I put my "Quick Fuse Seascape technique to the advanced test. Could I wow the quilting world with this basic concept? Was it enough to get people to say "Who is that dude?" Would quilters want to learn a new way to cheat the long, tedious process of appliqué quiltmaking? Oh did they ever. I still credit Alex Anderson and Simply Quilts for the biggest seven minutes of fame a guy could wish for. Even today when the show reruns, I still get emails asking for more detailed instructions. So, for the first time in print here is the total breakdown of the steps to "Beyond The Tides".

"The Concept" as seen in the previous versions of the Quick Fuse Seascape Quilt Photos and diagrams, there are two very important atmospheres. However, I wanted to duplicate the feel of the predetermined photo, so unlike most of my quilts I needed to draft a pattern.

I simply imported the photograph into Adobe Photoshop, and converted it to a grayscale image. This helps me to see the major tracing lines of the objects such as the big rocks. I knew I could get the feel for the scene without drafting every little piece, but the major shapes were important. I will try to not confuse the matter, but I printed out the new image to real size for the quilt, and illuminated the large photo with a light table so that I could trace the pieces to be from the backside of the new photo. Why you ask? Fusible webs will transpose the images due to they way they work, so if the image has a definite direction, then you must create an opposite for your tracings, by tracing the reverse of the pattern.

I know, I have been telling you all to just create the canvas first and not to worry about the appliqués, but there comes a time in a man's life when he must do the opposite of what he says. I needed the rock patterns, so I could figure the size of the strips of background fabrics that became the canvas. As a matter of fact, the quilt was only a rendering of the photo at first, there was no underwater portion in the original in the line up. When I had the layout set up, I realized that I could do so much more with the fabrics and the scene, that I decided to go beyond the photo, "Beyond the Tides". That is how the quilt found its name.

Step 1 The 'Canvas' - or the grouping of materials that will be sewn together in strips to form the background of the quilt. These fabrics make up the color story of the project to be, as well as set the scale and perspective for the appliqués. Choose these fabrics quickly so that you are trusting your artistic instinct.. The fabrics will be pieced as the background. Choose the fabrics that will appropriately depict the areas of seascape scene i.e. sky, ocean, etc. I constructed the underwater portion of the quilt quickly by using large scenic fabric prints. The fabric choices that are pieced into the canvas for below the waterline, need better the feel of the natural light of the scene, so consider this as you select and sew your cloth. Create the entire canvas with your sky, surface water(s), and the underwater fabrics.

Tip: Muslin is not used for the foundation.

Step 2 The 'Applique' - Once the background is pieced, with or without borders, begin the appliqué process. Choose your favorite fusible web and follow the manufacturer's instructions for use. Each product is similar, but may have slightly different ironing times and settings.

I prep as many appliqués as I can stand to cut in one sitting. Then to fight chair rot, I get up and start to position the appliqués into place. I never remove the paper from the appliqués until I am sure that the pieces are cut to fit just right. The larger the quilt the more the cutting. This process should not be rushed. Take the time to get the appliqués looking perfect. The appliqués are the paint on the canvas, they create the magic. I too often get three quarters of the appliqués done, and feel as if the quilt will never be finished. Then, out of the blue, one appliqué in the correct position, creates harmony in the quilt, and the project and you agree it is now complete.

A few more tricks:

- ☯ Consider ways to hide or soften the seam lines in the seascape. The rocks and waves were created from selected fabrics. Build up reefs under the tides.

- ☯ Fussy cut pieces from the same fabric as the background. This will trick the eye into believing the whole quilt is one big cheater panel. Hand dyed fabrics or fabric blends can be used to create rocks and individual coral pieces, as well as waves and white waters.

- ☯ Fussy cut prints from selected fabrics to enhance the ocean and reef.

Now the Quilting.

Use the machine's needle and thread to bring relief to the quilt, make your textures, and create your movement. The trick is to quilt around everything. Anchor the appliqués in the quilting process, raw edge appliqué style. This means, every object is outline quilted on the appliqué.

Quilt around all of the printed objects from the background fabrics that still show through from the appliqués. This will make the viewer assume that the entire quilt top is appliqués. From two feet away, you never know that only some the images have been fussy-cut appliquéd.

Free motion quilt the remaining background to stabilize the quilt as well as embellish the quilt. When finished most people think the quilt is a painting that has been quilted. Create borders that resemble frame matting. I always add a signature label and tabs to show the bamboo rod for hanging on the wall.

The original photo as sent to the participants of the Landscape Challenge.

My interpretation of the photo as set for making a pattern for the rocks.

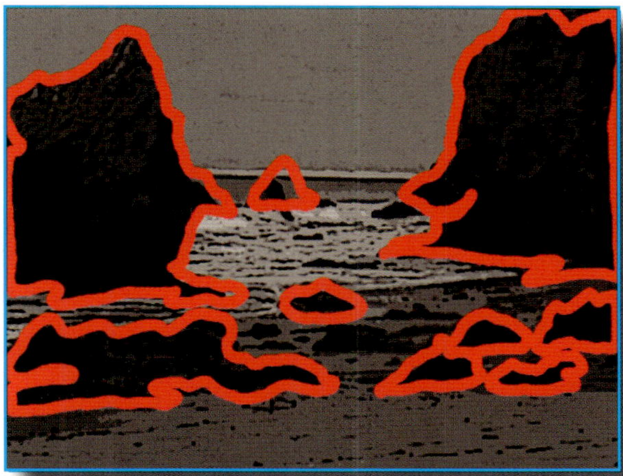

The center of the underwater portion of the quilt - hard to imagine it is not all one panel?

A nice Right handed wave breaking off of the rock appliqué.

A school of fish swimming through the appliqué of the underwater rocks that connect to the surface.

Glossary

- Appliqué – The process of creating a fabric image to set on the top of your canvas or quilt top.

- Backside – Facing away from the wave, your buns to the wave. The Back of the quilt or wrong side of the fabric.

- Batik – AKA Bali prints or tie dyes. Fabric that is dyed, not printed and usually has a variety of color and visual texture.

- Canvas – The grouping of fabrics that have been stitched together to make up the background for your scene.

- Duck Dive – pushing your surfboard and body under the oncoming white wash of the wave.

- Feed dogs – A job for a kennel worker. Also... little teeth that move the fabric under your sewing machine's presser foot.

- Front side - Facing the wave, your chest to the wave. The top of the Quilt or the Print side of your fabric

- Fussy Cut – Creating an appliqué by cutting along the printed line of an object in the fabric.

- Line Up – the group of guys in the ocean waiting for the set waves to come.

- Paddle Out – the process of trying to get you and your surf board to the waves.

- Quilt Police – the clever term for those who are so confident about their work they feel free to find fault in yours. No, they do not carry badges, but you will be able to spot one from a mile away.

Glossary

- Sandwich – The primary food sold at Subway® restaurants. Also... in the quilting world, to layer the quilt back, batting, and quilt top.
- Satin Stitch – a very narrow, tight zigzag stitch.
- Set Waves – the waves you want to surf.
- Transposed – Horizontal mirror image flip.
- Trapunto – To bring relief to a portion of your quilt or an appliqué by adding additional batting, only quilting the outline, then heavily quilting the area around the outline, leaving the portion raised. I suggest you look it up elsewhere, I cannot be expected to know everything...

- Brings a fresh, young feel to his quilts.
- Specializes in quilted seascapes.
- All man and machine made.
- Designed fabric line for Free Spirit Fabrics entitled "Florals and Corals".
- Designed and created over 35 quilts in the past three years.
- Has his own line of quilt patterns in a variety of technique styles.
- Teaches one-day classes.
- Hosts and instructs at 4 day quilting retreats (Fall & Spring)
- Does sales and service for Pfaff sewing machines.
- Is the Manager of the Cotton Ball, a sewing machine and quilt shop in Morro Bay.
- Will do commissioned projects; working with the customer on theme and color choices.
- Designs quilts for Michael Miller Fabrics, New York.
- Has recently sold quilts at the "Nature Quest Art Gallery".
- Is a sponsored Quilt Artist for Pfaff Sewing Machines
- Is a featured Artist on Simply Quilts with Alex Anderson.
- Is a Licensed Fabric designer for Telegraph Road Studios.
- Is a Licensed Embroidery Designer for Cactus Punch.

The story goes something like this...

I started working in my mother's quilt shop – "The Cotton Ball" in Morro Bay, California. My wife was working on a teaching credential so I needed to pick up some extra hours around the shop. We shortly then after became Pfaff sewing machine dealers, and that is when I became a quilter.

I first made about thirty aloha shirts, which yielded a fantastic wardrobe and a ton of scraps mostly batik and floral. This pile of stash and the eagerness to try free motion machine quilting became my first quilt, which now serves as a curtain in an office no one uses. My second quilt was the hit – "The Dolphin Dance" an easy strip pieced quilt that has sold over 600 patterns in my store alone and countless kits. I caught the quilt pox and was never cured. I began teaching myself to quilt through traditional techniques adapted for a man and his machine. Quilted Seascapes became my middle name.

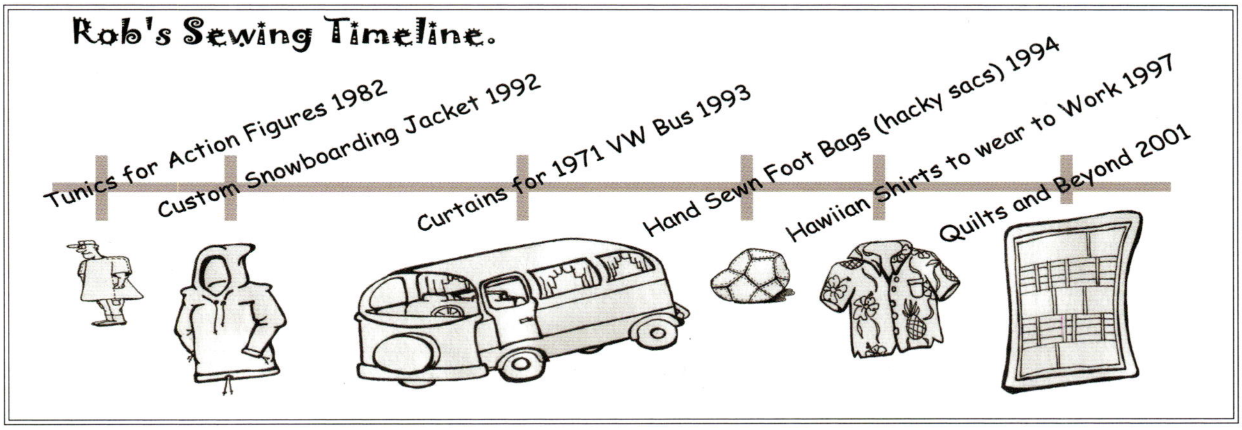

I began teaching my techniques in classes at our store, then four day quilting retreats. Somewhere along the line of trips to Houston Quilt Market I made a wise crack to the President of Free Spirit Fabrics and landed my first job as a fabric designer. Another wise crack and I was designing quilts for Michael Miller Fabric's new releases. I also was offered to show my quilts in a Marine Art Gallery. My opening was a huge success, selling a third of my hangings in the first weekend, and I hooked a commission quilt that now hangs in our county's most prestigious health club.

This story travels with me as I present my quilts and techniques to Guilds across California. I have taped for both Simply Quilts and Uncommon Threads in the past year, and things are just getting off the ground for me. Life is too short, be creative, have fun...and make some waves.

Rob with his family in Costa Rica... making waves.

Now a place to start your quilt, notes, or doodles...